Into The Cave With Mr. McDoogle

Written and Illustrated By:

Marie Whitton

For My Husband
Greg

For My Children
Gregory, Ann-Marie &
Kimberly

For My
Grandchildren

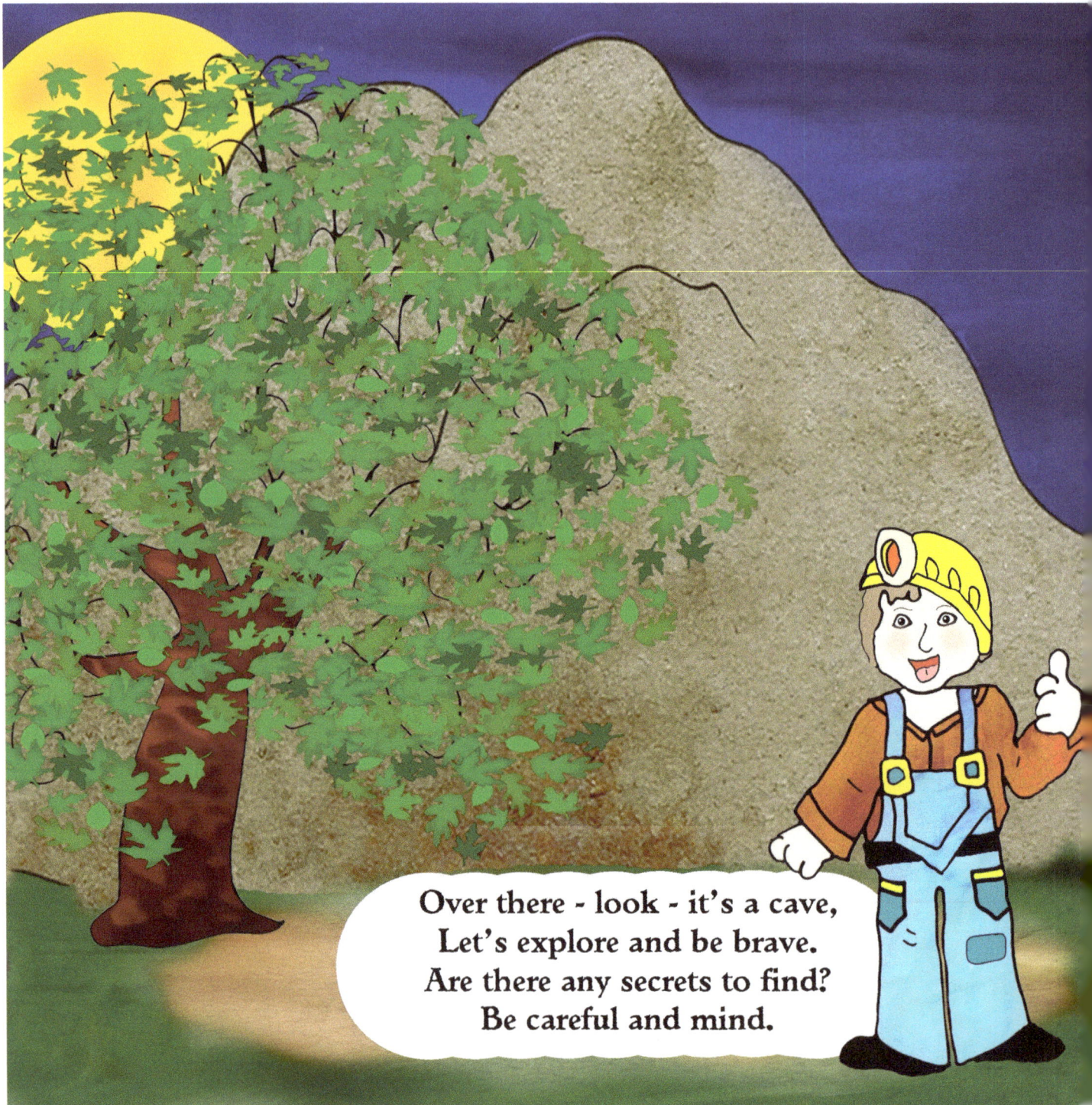

Over there - look - it's a cave,
Let's explore and be brave.
Are there any secrets to find?
Be careful and mind.

To protect from winter cold to summer swelter,
This cave was and is a shelter
From now to long ago,
These wall pictures do show.

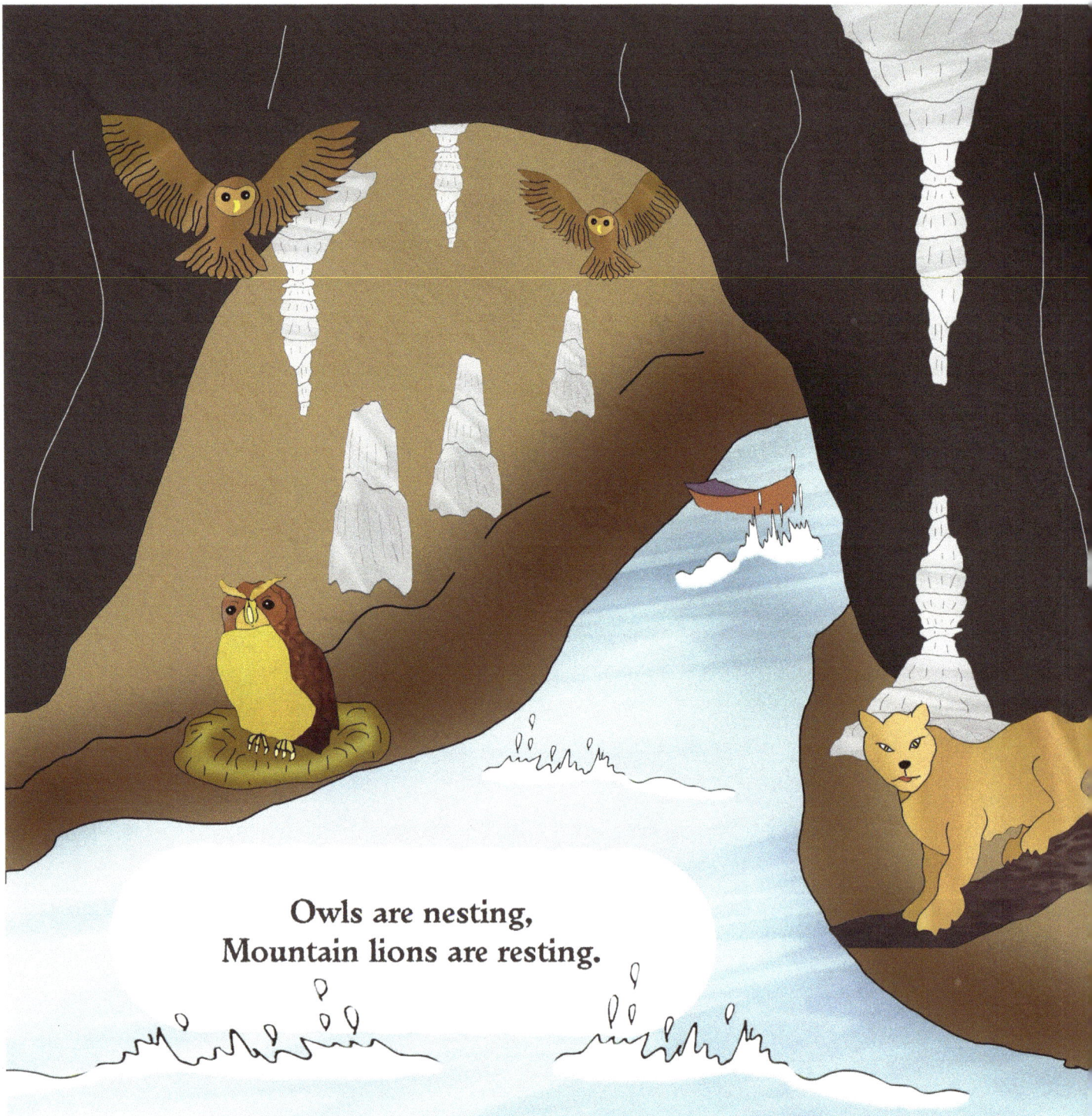

Owls are nesting,
Mountain lions are resting.

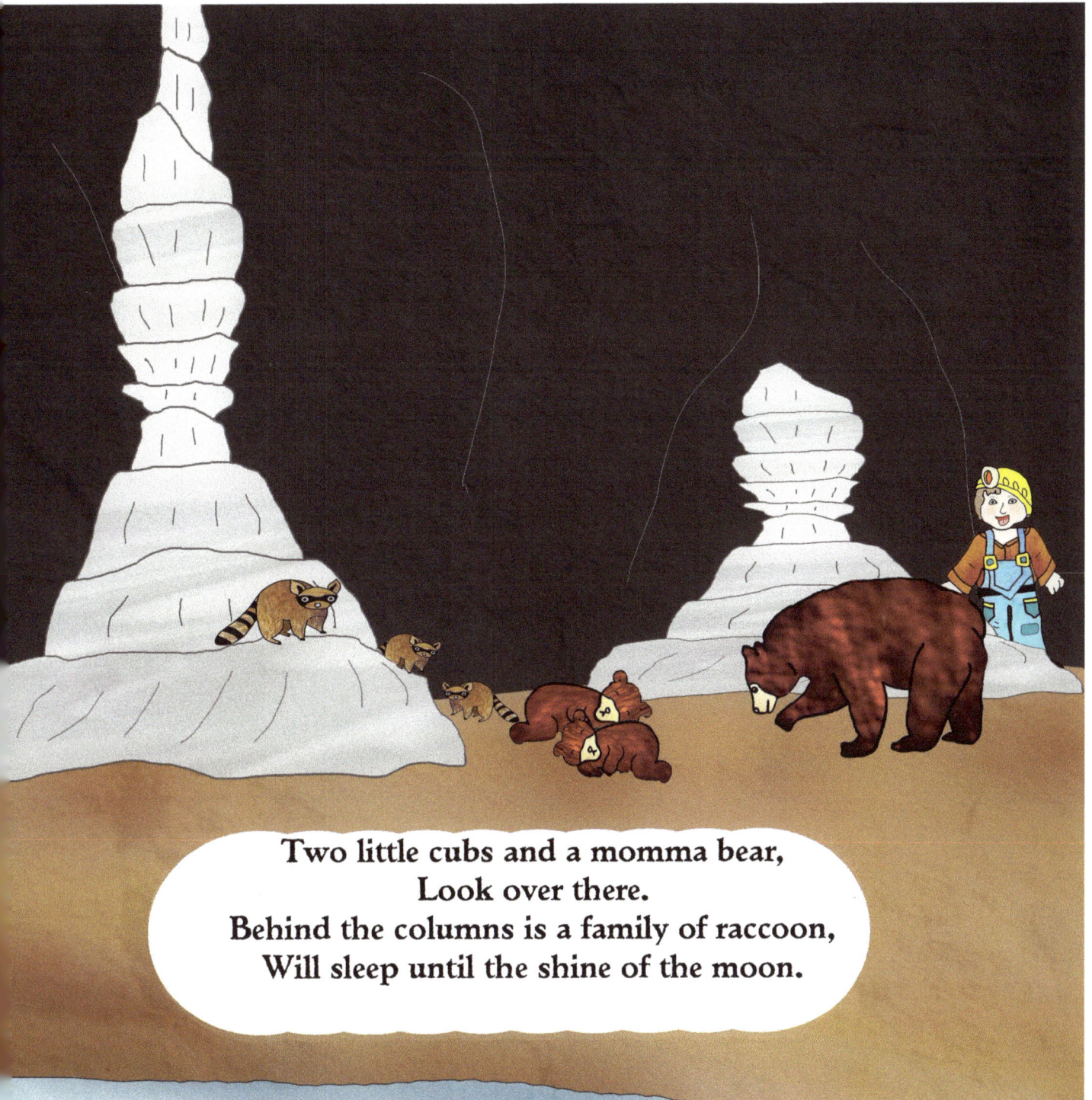

Two little cubs and a momma bear,
Look over there.
Behind the columns is a family of raccoon,
Will sleep until the shine of the moon.

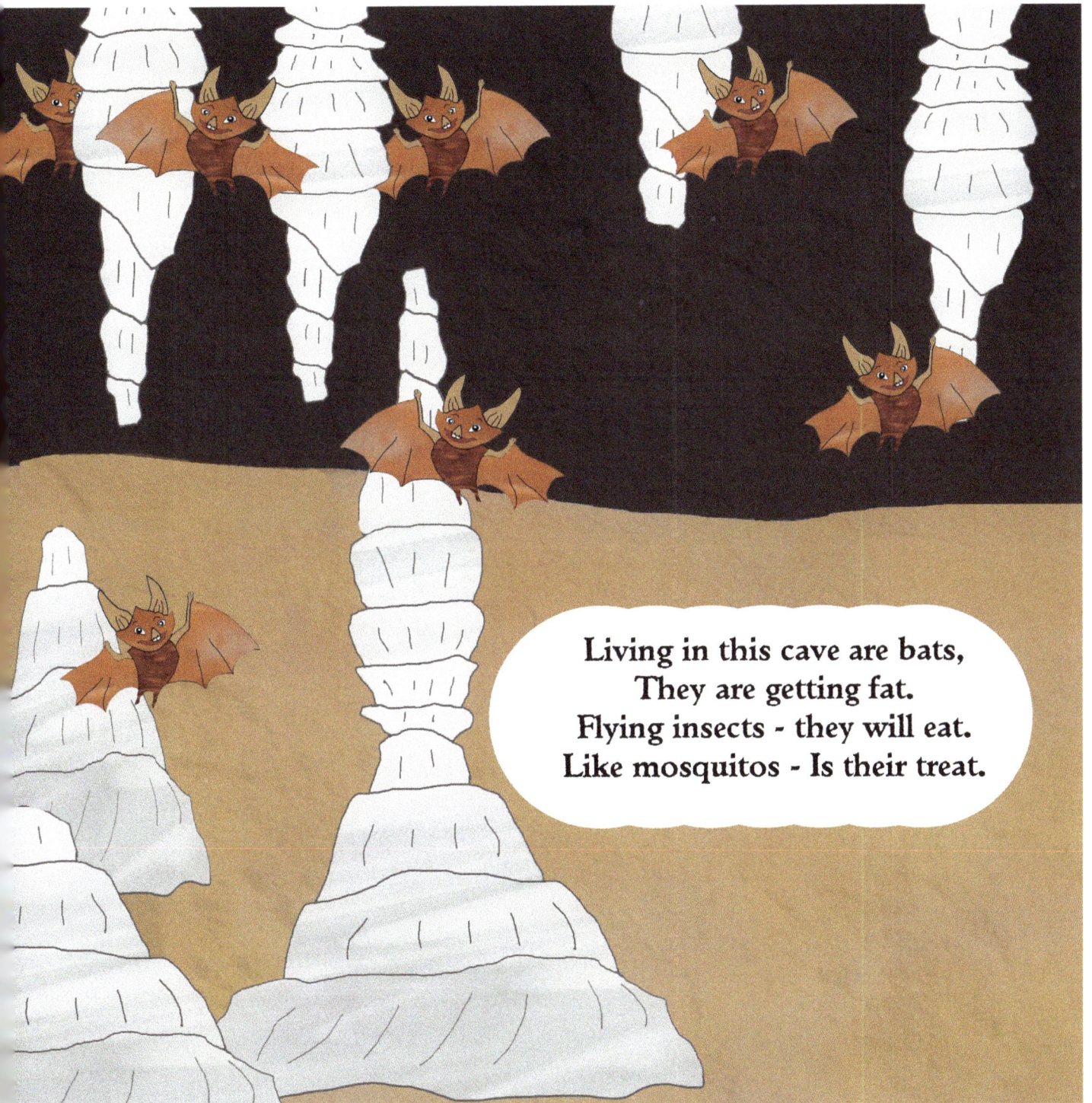

Living in this cave are bats,
They are getting fat.
Flying insects - they will eat.
Like mosquitos - Is their treat.

Mr. McDoogle turned out the light,
What a fright.
Can't see the hand in front of your face,
In this place.
This cave is sooooo dark,
All you hear are children's voices for a lark.

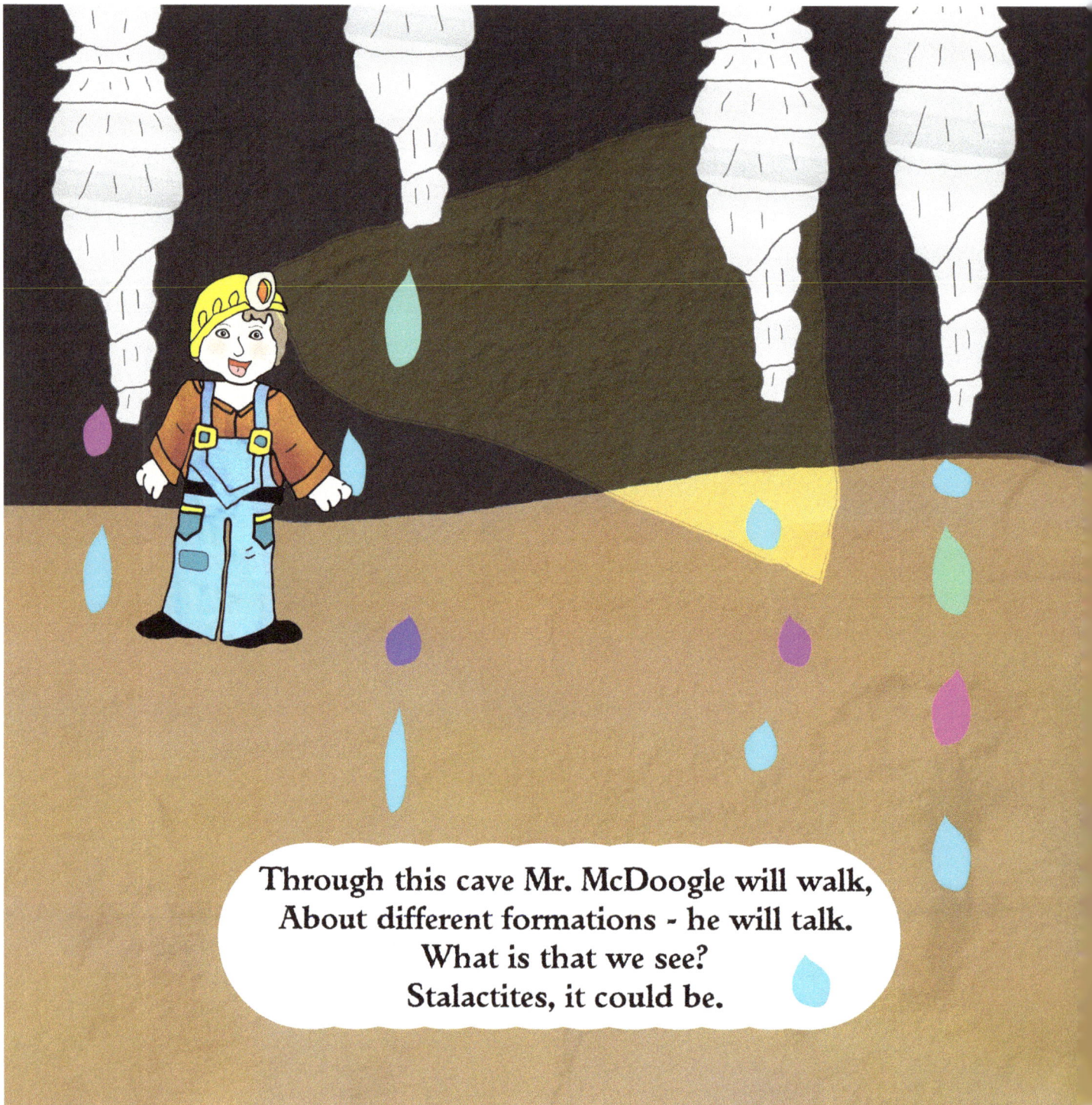

Through this cave Mr. McDoogle will walk,
About different formations - he will talk.
What is that we see?
Stalactites, it could be.

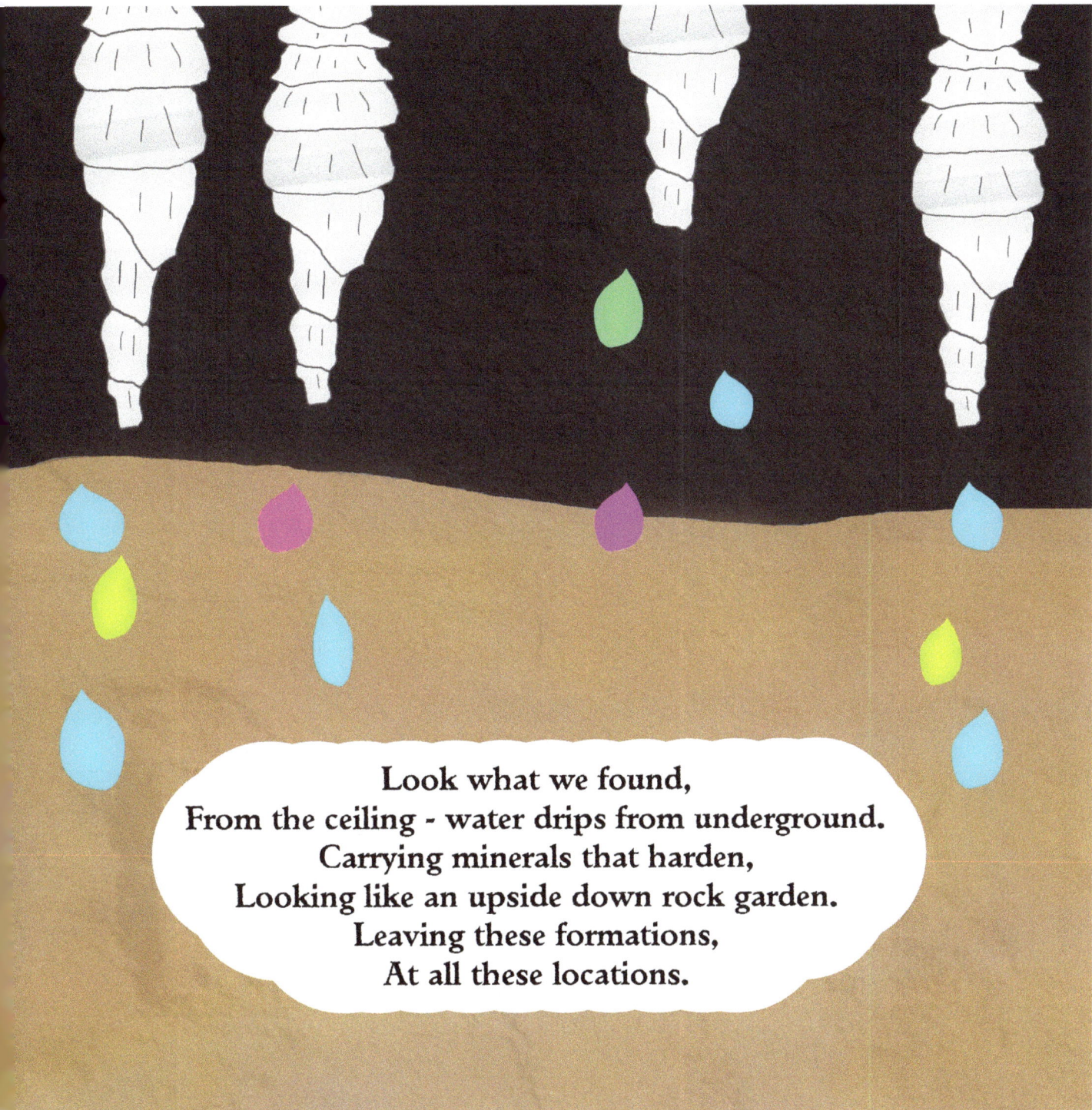

Look what we found,
From the ceiling - water drips from underground.
Carrying minerals that harden,
Looking like an upside down rock garden.
Leaving these formations,
At all these locations.

Next we see - growing on the floor - Stalagmites,
Water mixed with minerals drips off the Stalactites.

(trick to remember StalaGmites - from the Ground)
(StalaCtites - from the Ceiling)

Walking a little farther - A column - we will find,
A stalactite and stalagmite grow together to bind.
These formations - every 100 years - an inch will grow,
Very Very Slow.

Let's look for creatures,
Do they have any odd features?
Bugs and Salamanders - here are some,
They all look so glum.

So dark - fish have no eyes,
But they are wise.
What do they eat?
Dead bugs and plants at their feet.

Mr. McDoogle found a treasure,
What a pleasure.
He found silver and gold,
To much to hold.

These crystals are over 500,000 years old.
This is what Mr. McDoogle was told.
Magma keeps water temperature at 122 degrees,
Crystals grow from gypsum and minerals with ease.
Crystals grow to a very large size,
So large he can't believe his eyes.

Lots of secrets in this cave,
We explored and were brave.
A different world under-ground,
This is what we found.

www.ingramcontent.com/pod-product-compliance
Lightning Source LLC
Chambersburg PA
CBHW060754150426
42811CB00058B/1407